ACADIA
National Park

by Ruth Radlauer

**Photographs by
Ed and Ruth Radlauer**

**Design and map by
Rolf Zillmer**

AN ELK GROVE BOOK

 CHILDRENS PRESS, CHICAGO

To the naturalists,
who give Acadia National Park
its own special character.

With special thanks to Mr. Robert Rothe,
Park Naturalist, for his help
in preparing the manuscript for this book.

Cover Photo: Otter Cove From Western Point

Library of Congress Cataloging in Publication Data

Radlauer, Ruth Shaw.
    Acadia National Park.
    (Parks for people)
    "An Elk Grove book."
    SUMMARY: Presents the geography, plant and animal
life, and distinctive features of this national park on
the coast of Maine.
    1. Acadia National Park—Juvenile literature.
[1. Acadia National Park. 2. National parks and
reserves] I. Radlauer, Edward. II. Title.
F27.M9R3 1978   917.41'45   77-18056
ISBN 0-516-07495-4

Contents

What Is Acadia National Park?

Acadia National Park is a place of change. Over thousands of years it has changed. And it is still changing from year to year, day to day, and minute to minute.

Even while you visit, Acadia changes. One moment it's a breath of fresh air from a mountaintop that overlooks lakes, bays, and a fjord. Then it's the smell of balsam fir on a wooded trail or the rich, earthy smell of leaf mold on a springy forest floor.

Acadia is changing colors. Sometimes the blue sky is reflected in the water. But both water and sky may change quickly to gray, when islands seem to float on a fog that sneaks in from nowhere.

On shore, pink granite rocks change when ocean waves splash white against them. The rocks turn green, dark red, brown, and white as algae, barnacles, and other sealife cling to their roughness.

Here is an island dotted with lakes and topped with trees. It's being changed every minute by the constant work of weather, wind, and waves. This is your park, the everchanging Acadia National Park.

Fjords Are Made By Glaciers—Somes Sound

Wooded Trail—Acadia Mountain

Porcupine Islands Seen From Hulls Cove

Pea-Sized Acorn Barnacles

Your Trip to Acadia

Acadia National Park is in the northeast corner of the United States. Most of the park is on Mount Desert Island along with Bar Harbor, Maine, and other towns and villages. Schoodic Peninsula to the east and Isle au Haut about 27 kilometers to the southwest are outposts of the park.

Most people drive, but you can take a bus or fly to Bangor or Bar Harbor. Interstate Highway 95 leads to Bangor, Maine, and from there, U.S. 1 and State Route 3 take you to Ellsworth and Bar Harbor.

In the park you can stay as long as 14 days at Seawall or Blackwoods Campgrounds. Campsites have tables, benches, fireplaces, and restrooms nearby. There are no wilderness campsites for overnight backpacking.

The park is open all year, but most people visit in July and August when more activities are offered. Six months before your trip, write for information to the Superintendent, Acadia National Park, Bar Harbor, Maine, 04609. If campground reservations are filled, write to the chambers of commerce in Bar Harbor, Northeast Harbor, 04662, and Southwest Harbor, 04679, for information about campgrounds, motels, and cottages.

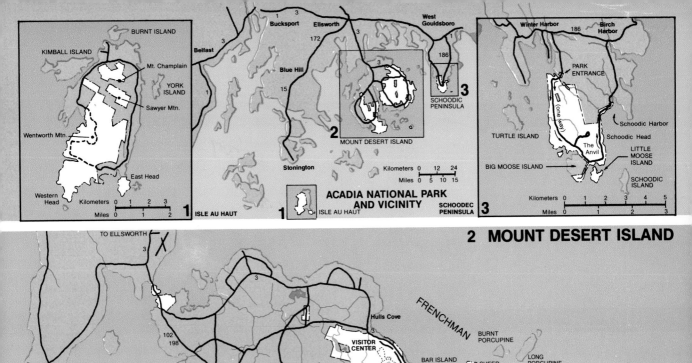
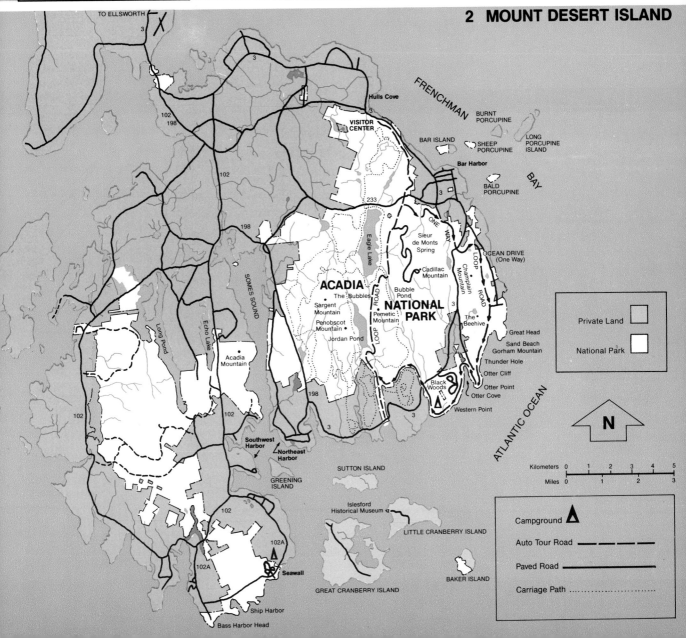

Islands from Mountaintops

When you visit Acadia National Park, try to imagine how it has changed in the last million years. About one million years ago, a range of mountains stood here at the edge of the land, or continent. But far to the north an ice age began. For many years, layers and layers of snow fell, and very little of it melted.

Slowly the snow packed into a huge mass of ice called a glacier. For hundreds of years the glacier grew. It spread south and covered much of North America. This continental glacier even covered the range of mountains. It scraped over the land, rounding off the mountains' peaks and gouging wide valleys.

Thousands of years passed, and the mountains sank under the weight of all that ice. When the glacier melted 12,000 to 15,000 years ago, only the mountaintops peeked above the water. The mountains had become a bare granite island with no soil for plants to grow.

How, then, did Acadia change into a national park covered with hundreds of kinds of trees, shrubs, and flowers?

Mount Desert Island From Baker Island ▶

Soil

On mountain hikes, you can find out how Acadia got its soil. Soil is made of sand mixed with tiny bits of decayed plants and animals.

Acadia's sand was formed by plant action and weathering. When water freezes in rock cracks, the ice makes the cracks wider. This breaks the rock into sand. Rocks are also made into sand when the pioneer plants, algae and fungi, combine to make lichens. Lichens make a weak acid that breaks down rock surfaces.

Sometimes sand washes into a dip or hollow. The hollow becomes a solution pit where decaying plants and animals mix with sand to make soil. When enough soil gathers in a solution pit, plants begin to grow in it. Mosses and ferns grow and die and grow, adding to the soil. This is called succession, and succession goes on as grasses and flowers start to grow. Shrubs and trees follow in the succession, and they add to the soil.

In Acadia National Park, the soil changes from place to place. Here and there soil collects, mixes with decayed things, and gets deep and rich. In other areas the soil is thin because much of it blows or washes away.

New Plants Grow Where Soil Has Formed

Small Plants Cling To Thin Soil—Great Head

Gifts from the Soil

Because soil has formed on Mt. Desert Island, we receive the gift of plants. But they must adapt to different kinds of soil and many kinds of weather.

Plants that grow in thin, sandy soil would never grow in a bog where the soil is soggy with water. But the pitcher plant and round-leaf sundew adapt well in a bog because swarms of insects supply some of their food. The pitcher plant's flower and fruit stand tall on a thin stem. Its leaves, shaped like big cream pitchers, grow near the ground and hold water. Insects drown in this water, and the leaf gives off a juice that digests their soft parts.

Look very low on the ground of a bog to find the tiny plant called round-leaf sundew. Each sundew leaf is covered with sweet, sticky hairs. Insects are attracted to the leaves but soon find themselves stuck in the gooey hairs. When an insect struggles to get away, the leaf hairs bend over and trap it. Soon the insect dies, and the hairs give off a juice that digests it.

itcher Plant Blossom

Pitcher Plant Leaf

Round-Leaf Sundew

Mountain Flowers

As you walk up the mountainside, you see changes in the soil. At the base of the mountain, the ground is soft and springy. Spruce and balsam fir trees grow in an acid soil covered with needles and leaves. Because of the acid soil, needles and leaves decay more slowly, so they form a thick cushion. When this cushion decays, it forms a rich part of the soil called humus or duff.

During July, in sunnier parts of the forest, the ground is covered with the red berries of bunchberry dogwood. In damp soil, the shrub meadowsweet reaches its white or pink blossoms to the sun.

High up the mountain, the soil is thinner and fewer trees grow. In some places the soil has been washed off the granite rocks. But here and there an American harebell finds a bit of soil between boulders. It pushes its blue bell out for you to see.

Near the top, if you look very carefully in protected hollows, you may find the blooms of bright red wood lilies swaying on tall stems.

nchberry Dogwood

Meadowsweet

od Lily—Great Head Summit

A New Forest

On a hike up these mountains, you'll see changes in the trees. Near the ocean, white spruce grow in spite of the drying effects of wind and salt spray. Up from the shore, red spruce and fir trees grow in thicker, wetter soil.

High on the mountains, the warm growing season is short. Cold winds dry the soil and plants. Pitch pines hold their cones until they're ripe enough to drop their seeds. The wind turns some into flag trees with branches growing to one side.

In October of 1947, a strong wind whipped a fire out of a burning peat bog into the forest. The fire traveled ten miles in two hours. After the fire, over 67 square kilometers of evergreen trees had turned to black skeletons.

Since that time, a succession of plants has created a new forest. First to grow were low shrubs and the broadleaf trees—aspen, maple, and birch. Years later small evergreens such as pines, firs, and spruces sprang up in the shade of the broadleaf trees. These will grow tall and crowd out the aspens and others. A new evergreen forest will have grown in the ashes of the old one.

ag Trees—Acadia Mountain

wo Years of Cones—Pitch Pine

Birch Trees Grow First—Great Head

The First Summer Visitors

The first people to enjoy the place now known as Acadia were the Abnaki Indians. In birch bark canoes, they came down the rivers and across to Mount Desert Island. Some say they came in summer to escape the mosquitoes and black flies of the mainland woods.

The Indians fished and dug clams to eat. Their campsites are marked by heaps of clam shells. Hundreds of years later, scientists dug into these shell heaps. They found tools made of bone and stone and baskets made of grasses and birch bark.

You can see many of these artifacts in the Abbe Museum at Sieur de Monts Spring. This is a spring where Indians got their fresh water and where a later landowner built a springhouse. Nearby at the Nature Center, you can taste the clear, cool water that bubbles up where Indians once drank.

Today Sieur de Monts Spring also has a nature display called the Wild Garden. Here a private group has gathered many of Acadia's native plants from beach, bog, and mountains. It's a good place to learn about the plants you've wondered about as you hiked all over the island.

Stone Tools—Abbe Museum Of Stone Age Antiquities

rtifacts—Grass And Birch Bark

Springhouse—Sieur De Monts Spring

The
Next Visitors

After the Indians came Europeans from across the sea. In 1604 the French explorer Champlain sailed by and saw an island with almost no trees. He named it *L'isle des Monts Deserts,* French for *The Island of Desert Mountains.* In 1604 "desert" meant bare, or without trees.

Champlain claimed the island for the King of France, along with much of eastern Canada and the coast land as far south as New Jersey. But in 1606 the English claimed the same land for the Colony of Massachusetts. For about 150 years, France and England fought over Acadia or traded it back and forth. In 1775 it was held by the English, so after the Revolution it became American. But the island was really owned by descendants of earlier English and French owners.

You can hear more of this story if you take a boat cruise to visit the Islesford Historical Museum. VIPs (Volunteers In Parks) give the history and show you the spinning wheel and other things brought here by early settlers. You almost wish you could travel in one of the boats like the models in the museum.

esford Historical Museum—Little Cranberry Island

Model Boat—Islesford Museum

Baker Island

On a historic cruise to Baker Island, you can feel how it was to settle an island. The cruise starts on a ferry from Northeast Harbor. At Baker Island, you are rowed ashore in a rocking boat called a dory. Once you're on the island, a park naturalist tells how William and Hanna Gilley came here in 1806. They came all the way from the mainland in a dory. Packed into the tiny boat were their three children, some animals, tools, and household goods.

The forest and the ocean shaped their world as they farmed, fished, and hunted. They cleared the land and built a home with spruce trees. Hanna spun flax to make linen for clothes, and an older son made shoes for the family.

Hanna had nine more children and taught all 12 of them in the island's school. When a lighthouse was built there, William earned $350 a year keeping the oil lamps burning. The lighthouse was a welcome sight for fishing ships returning home.

As you dory to the ferry for the ride back, you may wish you could stay longer to search the tide pools and listen to the waves lapping the shore.

Dory To Baker Island From The Ferry

ker Island Lighthouse

Gifts from the Sea —Lobsters

At Acadia National Park, you hear a lot about the American lobster. This sea animal has its bones, or skeleton, on the outside. A lobster has two big claws, each one different from the other. One claw has a crushing edge, and the other is a sharp grabber.

Lobsters are scavengers and cannibals. They eat almost anything, even smaller or weaker lobsters. Their sharp claws can cut another lobster in two.

A female lobster carries between 20,000 and 75,000 fertilized eggs under her tail for nine or ten months. When she frees the eggs, they hatch into lobsters no bigger than mosquitoes. They float near the top of the water for about 45 days.

As a lobster grows, its skeleton gets too tight. Then it molts, or sheds, its skeleton. A baby lobster molts about four times, then goes to the bottom of the sea. After 80 days and molting many times, a lobster is still only about 2½ centimeters long. When it's old enough to mate at five years, a lobster is over 26 centimeters long.

At the age of six, a female frees her first fertilized eggs. After that she produces eggs every other year.

American Lobster

Lobstering

Early settlers found many big lobsters crawling in shallows along the shore. They used them as cheap food for their servants or plowed lobsters and seaweed into the soil for fertilizer.

Today most people think lobster is a fine seafood. That's why you see so many bright-colored buoys floating on the waters around Acadia National Park. The buoys are tied by very long ropes to wooden traps sitting on the sandy bottom under the water. A lobster crawls into the trap to get the bait of rotting fish. Usually, the lobster cannot get out.

Every other day a lobsterman checks his traps. He looks for buoys of his own design and color. A license number is carved on each buoy. The lobsterman pulls each trap out of the water, throws back any lobsters that are too big or too small, and keeps those he can sell.

If a lobsterman finds a female with eggs, he puts a notch in her tail and puts her back in the water. If another person traps that female after she has freed her eggs, the notch tells him she must be returned to the sea. Her next batch of eggs will help to keep these waters supplied with more lobsters.

bster Trap Buoys

bster Traps, Or Pots

Lobster Boat

Gifts from People

In about 1880, people of the eastern states began to vacation along the coast of Maine. Many people built summer cottages on Mount Desert Island. Some of the cottages were very big and surrounded by a great deal of land.

People who loved the beauty of this island were afraid it might soon be covered with houses and hotels. They formed a group, bought up as much land as they could, and saved it for public use. The area became a national monument in 1916. Then in 1919, it became the first national park east of the Mississippi River.

After the 1947 fire, most people did not rebuild their summer cottages, but gave their land to the park. That's why you can come here today and roam through about 139 square kilometers of mountains, forests, lakes, and seashore. You'll find more than 80 kilometers of carriage roads set aside for bicycling, horseback riding, and hiking. Marked trails take you up and down the mountains and along the shores.

In summer months you can join in Star Watches from Cadillac Mountain, Bird Walks, and Night Prowls. All of these are guided by Park Naturalists and volunteers.

Acadia National Park—A Gift From People To People

Making the Most of Your Stay

Lakes, ponds, streams; bird walks, mountain hikes, boat cruises. There's much to see and do at Acadia. To make the most of your stay, go to the Visitor Center and plan. Here you can get a free map and summer schedule and buy a motorist guide. The guide explains the important things to see on a trip along Ocean Drive and Park Loop Road. Parking areas make stopping easy when you look at the Porcupine Islands in Frenchman Bay. Easy walks take you to Sand Beach, Thunder Hole, and Otter Point. When a wave rolls into Thunder Hole, it traps air and compresses it. When the air bursts out, it makes a big splash and a loud boom.

You can hike on your own or join any of the guided mountain hikes. But you must sign up for some activities, such as the Bird Walk or Geology Hike. You need good hiking shoes for all activities, and binoculars make a bird walk more fun.

All park activities are free except boat cruises and horseback rides. The schedule will tell how to sign up and pay for these.

Waiting For The Boom At Thunder Hole

Birds

If you have a reservation, you can go on an early-morning bird walk. The naturalist helps you spot birds with your binoculars. On a good day you may see a red crossbill, cedar waxwing, or any of the 275 kinds of birds that live in or visit Acadia.

Double-crested cormorants swim along the shore. Or you may see these big black birds flying low over the bay. They dive for fish and stay under water for a long time, chasing their dinner. Later, they perch on rocks and spread their wings to dry.

Three kinds of gulls fly around Acadia. The smallest with a black head is the laughing gull. The largest is the great black-backed gull. The most common is the herring gull. Since they are scavengers, one may swoop down to clean up your picnic.

During a cruise, you often see one or two of these scavengers following the boat. You always see them flying around lobster boats. They want to eat the old bait the lobstermen throw out each time they empty a trap. Gulls make good cleanup crews.

Double-Crested Cormorants

Herring Gull

The Tide Pool World

During high tide, water covers a whole world that lives among the rocks along the shore. At low tide, you can explore this watery world when you go on a tide pool walk with a park naturalist. The naturalist shows you many kinds of sea life, and then you can hunt for them in the tide pools.

As you walk carefully over the slippery seaweed, you may find a dog whelk. This is a snail that lives mostly in water, feeding on tiny animals.

If you find a crab, be sure to hold it from the back, so it can't pinch you.

Starfish eat other animals, even the mussel, locked tight in its two shells. The starfish pushes its stomach into the mussel and digests it right in the shell.

But starfish have enemies too; crabs and sea gulls. If an enemy grabs one of its arms, or rays, the starfish can let go of the ray. That's how a five-pointed star turns into a four-pointed one. But this lucky animal can grow a new ray where the old one dropped off.

All of these animals can only live in the very cold waters of Acadia. So, of course, you put them back in the water after you've had a good look.

ide Pool Walk

Dog Whelk

ock Crab

Starfish, Big And Little

Other Animals

Many other animals live in Acadia, but they're not as easy to see. Most animals protect themselves by hiding or by going out only at night.

After the sun goes down, the beaver comes out of its lodge and swims to the edge of the pond. It may cut aspen or willow trees to add to the beaver lodge or dam. In fall, beavers store tree branches and twigs under the water for a winter supply of food.

From the top of Cadillac Mountain, you can look down at the valley below and see the work of beavers.

But you must be out early in the morning to spot the snowshoe or varying hare. Its big feet give this animal one of its names. Because its feet are big like snowshoes, it can walk across the snow without sinking in too deep.

This cousin of the rabbit is also called a varying hare because the color of its coat changes, or varies. In summer, a brown coat helps the hare hide among plants. As fall turns to winter, the hare sheds its brown fur and grows a white coat. Then the hare is protected from its enemies who cannot see it against the snow-covered ground.

Snowshoe Hare In Summer Coat ▶

What's That?

You'll probably have many questions about this and that in Acadia. On a young persons' walk, everyone asks, "What's that?" Sometimes you think about just one question like, "What is a hole?" It's fun because there are many answers. Maybe a hole is nothing. But some holes are homes—chipmunk homes in the ground or bird homes in tree trunk holes.

Or the question is, "What is a rock?" Then you talk about how the granite rocks of this island formed. And someone asks about the balanced boulder. How do scientists know a glacier brought it to the South Bubble from a place more than 32 kilometers to the north?

Often the leader brings small rocks from OUTSIDE THE PARK, so you can pick one for your own. With eyes closed, you "get to know" your rock. Then the rocks are passed around the circle. By feeling each one, you try to find your own.

Finally, you get to make your rock "live" with color markers. Some make their rocks look like faces. Others turn them into designs.

After one of these walks, you go away asking more questions. And you'll see much more in the holes and rocks of Acadia National Park.

Balance Boulder Brought Here By A Glacier

Find Your Own Rock

Make The Rock Live

Mountain Hikes

You find out a lot more about rocks on any of the mountain hikes. The Geology Hike starts at Sand Beach where you pick up the sand and study its tiny grains. About half the grains are ground-up rocks. The other half are broken shells.

Then you hear how hot, molten rock, called magma pushed up under other layered rocks. The magma cooled and became granite. Later the glacier scraped away most of the layered rock and changed the peaks into lower granite mountains.

There are other signs of the glacier's visit on Acadia Mountain. From the top you look down on Somes Sound, a fjord, or basin, carved out by a glacier and filled with sea water. You see where the glacier moved along, carrying rocks and sand beneath it. Under the weight of the ice, rocks cut deep scratches, or glacial grooves, in the granite. Sand beneath the glacier ground away and polished the rock, making it smooth.

This is one of the few places in Acadia to find glacial grooves and polish. The others have weathered and eroded away from this constantly changing island.

The Fjord, Somes Sound, From Acadia Mountain

Glacial Grooves

Which Way? Orienteering

Acadia's mountain trails are marked, so you can't get lost. But if you learn to use a map and compass, you should never lose your way.

You can learn to use a map and compass if you go orienteering with a park naturalist. First you learn to read a topo, or topographic, map. You find out that contour lines tell how steep a hill is. Special symbols tell where streams and marshes are. Other symbols mark schools and churches.

Next you learn the parts of a compass and what the different arrows mean. With information from your map, you correct your compass to help you find true north. Then you learn how to hold the compass and which arrow points the way to go.

Once you get deep into the forest with a partner, you may feel quite sure your compass is wrong. But you remember what the naturalist said: "Trust your compass." So you keep orienteering the way you were told. And when you reach the target, the place you're supposed to find, you decide you can trust your compass—when you've learned how to use it.

Correct The Compass

Take A Reading From The Map

Find Your Way Through The Forest

Your Changing Park

Acadia National Park always changes. It has grown from a national monument of 24 square kilometers to a national park of almost six times that size. Will it continue to grow? Will people donate more land, or will the government have a chance to buy more? How will the park change in the future?

Fire has changed Acadia. It destroyed about one third of the park's evergreen forest. Now a new forest of broadleaf trees grows in its place. They give more habitats for more animals. But later, the evergreens will grow tall again and crowd out the broadleaf trees.

Water changes Acadia all the time. Stormy winter waves lift big boulders out of the water and tumble them onto the shore. Waves carry most of the grains of Sand Beach out to sea every winter. Even after the sand washes back in spring, it is shifted about by wind and water.

Anemone Cave and Thunder Hole, carved by water, tell the story of an endless battle between land and sea.

You can be sure of one thing. You'll find a different place each time you return to Acadia National Park.

Sunset Over Great Cranberry Island ▶

Other National Parks in the East

In 1919, Acadia became the first national park in the east. Then in 1940, GREAT SMOKY MOUNTAINS NATIONAL PARK was dedicated. Preserved in this park are farms of the early settlers of Tennessee and North Carolina. Nature's finest artistry paints this park with wild flowers in spring and fiery colored leaves in the autumn.

MAMMOTH CAVE NATIONAL PARK has within its boundaries the longest cave in the world. Many different tours from easy to very hard take visitors through the cave. Hikes and nature walks offer a topside view of a vast hardwood forest, wild flowers, and some animals.

EVERGLADES NATIONAL PARK is a flat-lying park, covered with sawgrass standing in water. The sawgrass plain is dotted with green humps which are hammocks, islands covered with mangrove and mahogany trees. Alligators, spiders, and colorful liguus snails live in the park. Beautiful big birds flock to this southern tip of Florida, making the Everglades a birdwatcher's dreamland.

able Mill—Great Smoky Mountains National Park

Lantern Tour—Mammoth Cave National Park

Egrets—Mrazek Pond—Everglades National Park

The Author and Illustrators

Wyoming-born Ruth Radlauer's love affair with national parks began in Yellowstone. During her younger years, she spent her summers in the Bighorn Mountains, in Yellowstone, or on Casper Mountain.

Ed and Ruth Radlauer, graduates of the University of California at Los Angeles, are authors of many books for young people. Along with their young adult daughter and sons, they photograph and write about a wide variety of subjects ranging from motorcycles to monkeys.

The Radlauers live in California, where Ruth and Ed spend most of their time in the mountains near Los Angeles.